CONTENTS

SCIENCE

JOBS IN SCIENCE

A QUALIFICATION IN SCIENCE CAN TAKE YOU FROM THE WILDS OF THE WORLD TO THE VERY EDGE OF SPACE!

Welcome to the world of working in science. Studying science is really worthwhile, because it opens doors to a whole range of interesting, exciting and unusual jobs — amazing jobs in science.

Studying science doesn't mean you'll be stuck in a lab. There are jobs in space, astronomy, sport and food production, to name a few. Find out what each job is all about, as well as the rewards of doing the job.

▼ Polar scientists provide vital data on the health and condition of the planet.

► Astronauts perform important scientific experiments in orbit.

SUBJECTS AND QUALIFICATIONS

For each job, we've shown what subjects you can study as you move through education from school to university and beyond, and what further training you would need. These are quite general because what you study for a particular qualification will change depending on which country you are in.

SCHOOL: Education up to about the age of 16

THE ROUTE TO

SENIOR SCHOOL: Education from about 16 to 18

A SCIENCE JOB

UNIVERSITY: Studying for an undergraduate degree and a post-graduate degree, such as a master's degree and a doctorate

▲ A science qualification could take you to one of the most prestigious colleges on the planet, such as the Massachusetts Institute of Technology in Boston, USA.

STEM STANDS FOR SCIENCE, TECHNOLOGY, ENGINEERING AND MATHS. AS SCIENCE, TECHNOLOGY, AND ENGINEERING INDUSTRIES GROW, THERE IS INCREASING DEMAND FOR PEOPLE WITH STEM SKILLS.

PLANET HUNTER

ARE YOU FASCINATED BY THE IDEA OF ALIEN LIFE? IF YOU ARE, THEN YOU'VE FOUND THE PERFECT JOB!

An exoplanet is a planet orbiting a star other than our Sun. As an exoplanet hunter, you would search for these distant worlds, work out how big they are, and how they move around their stars. This would tells us about how other solar systems in the Universe work.

Studying these other worlds also tells us about our own solar system, whether there are other solar systems that are similar to our own, or whether ours is out of the ordinary in some way. More importantly, hunting for exoplanets will tell us how common Earth-like planets are, and so tell us the chances of alien life existing.

BY MAY 2016, SCIENTISTS HAD IDENTIFIED NEARLY 5,000 POTENTIAL EXOPLANETS. NEARLY HALF OF THESE HAD BEEN DISCOVERED USING THE KEPLER SPACE OBSERVATORY.

WHAT YOU DO

As an exoplanet hunter, you would analyse data collected by some of the world's most powerful and sensitive telescopes. These telescopes, which are either in space, such as the Kepler Space Observatory (see right), or on Earth's surface, are pointed at thousands of stars in our galaxy. They detect the tiny changes in brightness as the planets pass in front of their stars, or if the star wobbles as the planet orbits it.

ASTROBIOLOGISTS STUDY EXOPLANETS TO SEE IF LIFE COULD SURVIVE ON THEM. AN ASTROBIOLOGIST IS AN EXPERT ON HOW LIFE CHANGES THE APPEARANCE OF A PLANET AND THE CHEMICALS IN ITS ATMOSPHERE.

WHERE YOU WORK

You would be working in a team with other scientists. This could be at a large space agency, such as NASA (National Aeronautics and Space Administration) or the ESA (European Space Agency), or in the astronomy department of a university. You would normally be in an office, but there would be opportunities to visit giant telescopes, which are often sited on remote mountaintops or in deserts.

UNIVERSITY: A degree in astrophysics, followed by research into stars and planets

▼ Launched in March 2009, the Kepler Space Observatory watches nearly 150,000 stars to see if they have exoplanets orbiting them.

▲ Exoplanets can be huge gas giants, much bigger than Jupiter, the largest planet in our solar system, or small, rocky worlds.

SENIOR SCHOOL: More physics and maths, and possibly astronomy

THE ROUTE TO PLANET HUNTING

SCHOOL: Physics and maths, and an interest in the night sky

CRIME FIGHTER

8

FORENSIC SCIENTISTS WILL TAKE BLOOD SAMPLES AS EVIDENCE AND STUDY HOW BLOOD HAS SPLATTERED TO FIND OUT WHAT HAPPENED AT A CRIME SCENE.

THIS JOB USES CUTTING EDGE SCIENCE TO SOLVE CRIMES AND CATCH THE BAD GUYS!

As a forensic scientist, you are trying to link criminal suspects to a crime. Forensic scientists help the police to bring the suspects to court and have them prosecuted. No two cases are the same, so this job is always varied and interesting.

Criminals often accidentally leave evidence of their visit at the scene of a crime, or unwittingly take evidence from the scene with them. It's your job to search for this evidence at the scene and on suspects. Then you have to analyse the evidence and try to find matches between the suspect and a crime scene.

FORENSIC ANTHROPOLOGY IS A SPECIAL BRANCH OF FORENSICS. FORENSIC ANTHROPOLOGISTS USE THEIR SPECIALIST KNOWLEDGE OF ANATOMY TO BUILD UP A 3-D IMAGE OF WHAT A DEAD PERSON PROBABLY LOOKED LIKE, USING THEIR SKULL AS A STARTING POINT.

▶ Forensic scientists catalogue and collect all sorts of evidence, such as footprints, fibres from clothing and traces of saliva.

WHAT YOU DO

What you do each day depends on the stage of a crime case, and your particular role in an investigation. At the start of a case, you might visit the scene of the crime to search for and collect evidence. This has to be carefully packaged and labelled. Most of the time you would be based in a forensic laboratory, using test equipment to analyse samples. This could involve looking at fibres under a microscope, analysing the different chemicals in a speck of paint, or sending a sample of blood to a laboratory for its DNA to be analysed. At the end of a case, you might be called to a court of law to act as an expert witness, telling the court about the evidence that you've found. So you need to be sure of your facts!

WHERE YOU WORK

As a forensic scientist, you would work for the police service in your country, in the forensic science section, or for a company that does forensic work for the police. Forensic scientists also work for fire services, helping to find out what caused a fire, or the armed forces, investigating crimes involving military personnel.

▶ Many police forces have specialist labs set up for their forensic teams.

THE ROUTE TO FORENSIC SCIENCE

SCHOOL: Science and maths

SENIOR SCHOOL: Physics and chemistry.

UNIVERSITY: A degree in chemistry, biology or medical science

AFTER UNIVERSITY: Specialist training in forensics

FEEDING THE WORLD

THIS JOB MAKES SURE THAT THE FOOD YOU EAT IS SAFE, NUTRITIONAL AND TASTY.

You only have to look at the ingredients and the information on food packaging to see that a great deal of science is involved in preparing your food. Food scientists use their knowledge of chemistry to develop tasty new things to eat and drink and improve the quality and taste of other food and drink products.

Food scientists also find out how to make food and drinks more quickly and cheaply, and how to make them last longer on supermarket shelves.

WHAT YOU DO

▼ Testing food to make sure it is safe and free from germs is a key part of a food scientist's job.

As a food scientist, you would work in a laboratory most of the time, trying different combinations of ingredients to create new foods. You might also organise tasting sessions to see how customers like the flavours of new products. If you are working in food production, you would spend time in a factory, carrying out quality and safety tests on finished products.

THE ROUTE TO FOOD SCIENCE

SCHOOL: Science and maths

▲ Governments have their own food testing labs, such as this one in Australia.

WHERE YOU WORK

There are plenty of opportunities for food scientists, as there are thousands of companies producing food and drink in most countries. These can range from small bakeries and chocolatiers to huge companies producing millions of ready meals for supermarkets. Some food scientists also work for local authorities as hygiene inspectors, taking samples of food from shops and restaurants to make sure they are safe to eat.

▲ Food scientists also calculate the nutritional information that goes on food packaging, so that shoppers can make an informed decision about their diet.

UNIVERSITY: A degree in food science

SENIOR SCHOOL: More science, especially chemistry

A FOOD FLAVOURIST USES CHEMISTRY TO CREATE BEAUTIFUL TASTES BY COMBINING DIFFERENT INGREDIENTS AND CHEMICALS. FLAVOURISTS WORK FOR COMPANIES CALLED FLAVOUR HOUSES.

WORKING IN SPACE

GET READY TO BLAST OFF WITH A JOB THAT IS TRULY OUT OF THIS WORLD.

An astronaut admires the view from the International Space Station.

As well as the thrill of living in space, and having an incredible view of Earth, astronauts push the boundaries of science and technology. A mission specialist is an astronaut who carries out a particular scientific or technical job in space. Each mission specialist has a list of jobs to do. These jobs include looking after a range of science experiments, such as testing how plants grow, or how crystals form in the low gravity of Earth's orbit. Other jobs include helping to maintain and repair the International Space Station (ISS).

WHAT YOU DO

As an astronaut, you will spend most of your time on Earth, training for your time in space. Once in space, you will sleep, eat and work to a strict timetable. Exercising on special machines is an important part of your day, to prevent your muscles from becoming weak in orbit.

◄ Training for a spacewalk involves many practice sessions underwater in a large pool back on Earth.

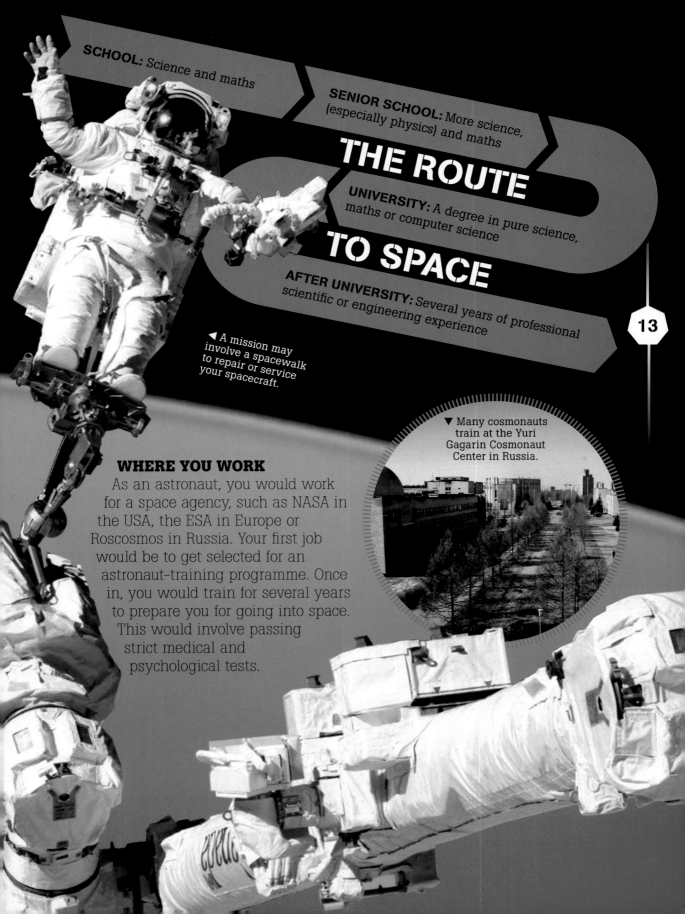

SCHOOL: Science and maths

SENIOR SCHOOL: More science, (especially physics) and maths

THE ROUTE

UNIVERSITY: A degree in pure science, maths or computer science

TO SPACE

AFTER UNIVERSITY: Several years of professional scientific or engineering experience

◀ A mission may involve a spacewalk to repair or service your spacecraft.

▼ Many cosmonauts train at the Yuri Gagarin Cosmonaut Center in Russia.

WHERE YOU WORK

As an astronaut, you would work for a space agency, such as NASA in the USA, the ESA in Europe or Roscosmos in Russia. Your first job would be to get selected for an astronaut-training programme. Once in, you would train for several years to prepare you for going into space. This would involve passing strict medical and psychological tests.

FIXING THE BRAIN

▼ A team of surgeons operate on the brain of a patient.

THIS JOB LETS YOU DELVE INTO THE MOST COMPLICATED MACHINE IN THE UNIVERSE – THE HUMAN BRAIN.

Being a neurosurgeon is one of the most challenging jobs in medicine. It requires amazing skills, takes a huge amount of training, and is very challenging. But it offers a huge amount of satisfaction in helping patients and saving lives.

Neurosurgeons treat patients who have problems with their nervous systems. They analyse what problems a patient has, decide whether they can fix them with an operation, and perform surgery if needed.

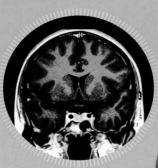

▲ Surgeons can study the inside of the brain using special scanners.

THE ROUTE TO NEUROSURGERY

SCHOOL: Sciences, especially biology

SENIOR SCHOOL: Biology and chemistry

CARDIOTHORACIC SURGERY INVOLVES THE HEART, LUNGS AND CHEST, INCLUDING CORRECTING HEART DEFECTS SUCH AS DAMAGED VALVES, AND HEART AND LUNG TRANSPLANTS.

YOUR BRAIN MAKES UP ABOUT 2 PER CENT OF YOUR WEIGHT, BUT USES 20 PER CENT OF YOUR BODY'S ENERGY.

WHAT YOU DO

As a neurosurgeon, you might have consultations with new patients to discuss their problems, organise tests (such as blood tests) and scans for them, decide treatment plans, and explain the plans to the patients. You would also do ward rounds, checking up on patients who are already undergoing treatment. You might also consult with a team to decide whether a particular patient needs surgery, and supervise more junior doctors. You would work in the operating theatre several hours a week, performing delicate surgery.

UNIVERSITY: A degree in medical science

AFTER UNIVERSITY: Five years general medical training, followed by up to ten years of specialist training while working as a doctor

WHERE YOU WORK

You would normally work for your country's health service, in a large hospital, possibly one that specialises in neurosurgery. Alternatively, you could work for a private health company.

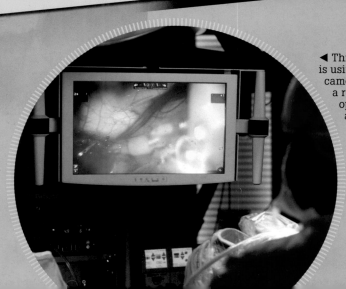

◀ This surgeon is using a TV camera and a robot to operate on a patient.

PENGUIN COUNTER

THIS SCIENCE JOB WILL TAKE YOU TO THE ENDS OF THE EARTH WHERE YOU CAN STUDY THE HEALTH OF OUR PLANET.

THE LARGEST PENGUIN COLONY CONTAINS ABOUT TWO MILLION CHINSTRAP PENGUINS. IT IS FOUND IN THE SOUTH SANDWICH ISLANDS.

A few scientists are lucky enough to work in some of the world's most beautiful places, including the polar regions.

As a polar scientist, you might study the climate, rocks, glaciers or the local wildlife. This work is important, as the changing numbers of penguins and other animals that live near the poles may be linked to human activities, and specifically to global warming.

Penguin researchers collect data, including how many birds live in each colony and how the numbers change over time. They attach small digital cameras and micro GPS trackers to some penguins to monitor their movements.

WHAT YOU DO

Counting penguins normally means leaving the cosy warmth of a polar base and living in a tent for weeks or even months, counting birds each day. The cold and wind, even in the Antarctic summer, make for difficult working and living conditions. But being in one the world's most beautiful places would offset these hardships. You will also spend time back at base analysing data.

▲ A team of scientists sets up instruments on the polar ice.

HERE'S ANOTHER SPECIALIST JOB IN THE ANTARCTIC OR ARCTIC. AN ICE-CORE DRILLER DRILLS DEEP DOWN INTO LAYERS OF ICE THAT HAVE BUILT UP OVER THOUSANDS OF YEARS. ANALYSING TINY BUBBLES OF AIR TRAPPED IN THE ICE CAN TELL US WHAT THE EARTH'S ATMOSPHERE WAS LIKE LONG AGO.

WHERE YOU WORK

You would be part a research organisation and work in a team that's based in the Antarctic for several months a year. You would spend the rest of your time back in the organisation's office, writing up research and preparing for future expeditions.

▼ The Amundsen–Scott Station at the South Pole.

THE ROUTE TO PENGUIN COUNTING

SCHOOL:
Sciences and maths

SENIOR SCHOOL:
Biology and maths

UNIVERSITY: A degree in biology or environmental science, followed by a master's degree or doctorate

STORM TRACKER

THIS JOB LETS YOU GET UP-CLOSE TO SOME OF THE MOST VIOLENT EVENTS ON THE PLANET.

Storm trackers are meteorologists who follow the progress of powerful storms, including hurricanes, tornadoes, and huge thunderstorms. They help us to predict dangerous storms and save lives by warning people to get out of the way.

Storm trackers monitor data from weather stations, images from satellites, and forecasts calculated by computers. This allows them to predict where storms may strike. Storm trackers occasionally study storms at close quarters. They might put themselves in the path of a hurricane or tornado to measure wind speeds and take photos.

▲ The winds in a tornado can reach speeds of more than 450 km/h.

THERE ARE ABOUT 1,000 TORNADOES EVERY YEAR ON AVERAGE IN THE UNITED STATES ALONE, AND ABOUT 100 IN CANADA.

WHAT YOU DO

As a storm tracker, you spend most of the time in an office, tracking hurricanes, or watching the development of storms that create floods or tornadoes. You might have to contact the media with storm warnings. On some days you might leave the office to collect data from the storm itself. In the case of a tornado, you'll be in a purpose-built truck equipped with radar wind-speed measuring equipment.

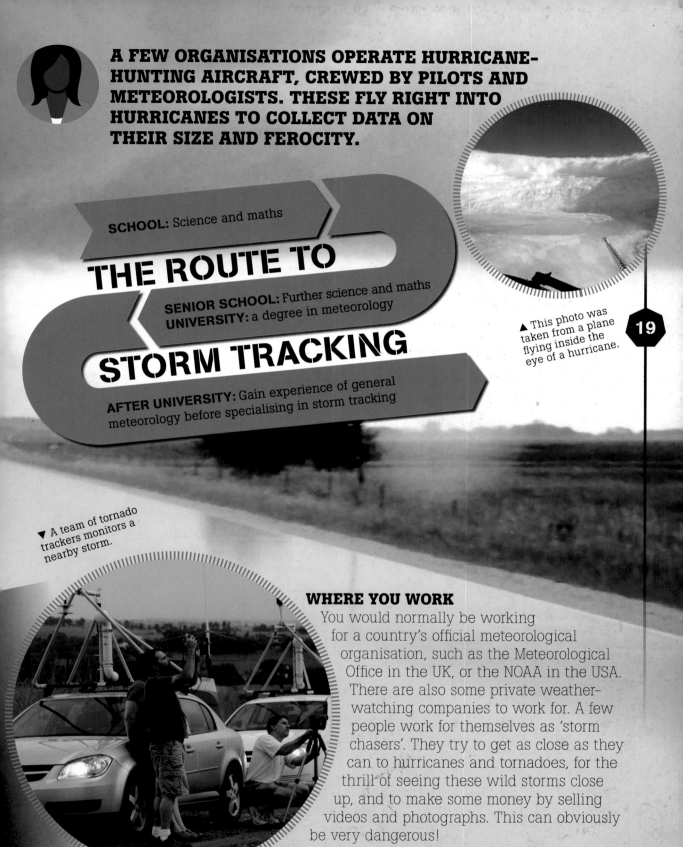

A FEW ORGANISATIONS OPERATE HURRICANE-HUNTING AIRCRAFT, CREWED BY PILOTS AND METEOROLOGISTS. THESE FLY RIGHT INTO HURRICANES TO COLLECT DATA ON THEIR SIZE AND FEROCITY.

THE ROUTE TO STORM TRACKING

SCHOOL: Science and maths

SENIOR SCHOOL: Further science and maths
UNIVERSITY: a degree in meteorology

AFTER UNIVERSITY: Gain experience of general meteorology before specialising in storm tracking

▲ This photo was taken from a plane flying inside the eye of a hurricane.

▼ A team of tornado trackers monitors a nearby storm.

WHERE YOU WORK

You would normally be working for a country's official meteorological organisation, such as the Meteorological Office in the UK, or the NOAA in the USA. There are also some private weather-watching companies to work for. A few people work for themselves as 'storm chasers'. They try to get as close as they can to hurricanes and tornadoes, for the thrill of seeing these wild storms close up, and to make some money by selling videos and photographs. This can obviously be very dangerous!

PREDICTING ERUPTIONS

THIS JOB MAY HAVE YOU PLAYING WITH FIRE, BUT IT'S VITAL TO PREDICTING ERUPTIONS AND SAVING LIVES!

Volcanologists observe volcanoes that are erupting, and monitor volcanoes that are dormant. They collect samples of ash and lava and record volcanic activity from hour to hour. They look for signs that dormant volcanoes are about to erupt again. These include the ground bulging, gases spewing from the volcano's vent, and small earthquakes that show that magma is moving deep underground. Volcanologists also look at the old lava flows and deposits of ash, which show them how volcanoes erupted in the past.

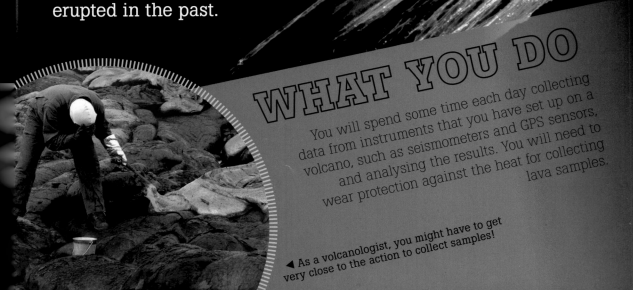

WHAT YOU DO

You will spend some time each day collecting data from instruments that you have set up on a volcano, such as seismometers and GPS sensors, and analysing the results. You will need to wear protection against the heat for collecting lava samples.

◄ As a volcanologist, you might have to get very close to the action to collect samples!

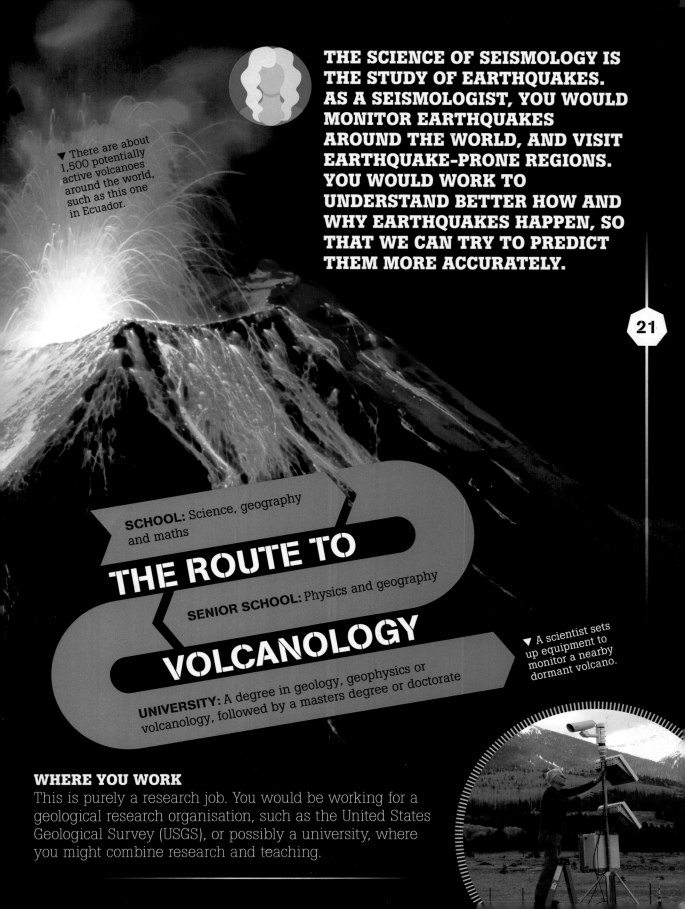

▼ There are about 1,500 potentially active volcanoes around the world, such as this one in Ecuador.

THE SCIENCE OF SEISMOLOGY IS THE STUDY OF EARTHQUAKES. AS A SEISMOLOGIST, YOU WOULD MONITOR EARTHQUAKES AROUND THE WORLD, AND VISIT EARTHQUAKE-PRONE REGIONS. YOU WOULD WORK TO UNDERSTAND BETTER HOW AND WHY EARTHQUAKES HAPPEN, SO THAT WE CAN TRY TO PREDICT THEM MORE ACCURATELY.

THE ROUTE TO VOLCANOLOGY

SCHOOL: Science, geography and maths

SENIOR SCHOOL: Physics and geography

UNIVERSITY: A degree in geology, geophysics or volcanology, followed by a masters degree or doctorate

▼ A scientist sets up equipment to monitor a nearby dormant volcano.

WHERE YOU WORK

This is purely a research job. You would be working for a geological research organisation, such as the United States Geological Survey (USGS), or possibly a university, where you might combine research and teaching.

GENETIC ENGINEER

SOME SCIENTISTS WORK WITH THE TINY BUILDING BLOCKS OF LIFE – GENES – TO CHANGE PLANT AND ANIMAL SPECIES.

DNA, or deoxyribonucleic acid, is a substance that's found in almost every cell in animals and plants. A gene is a chunk of DNA that controls how a particular cell grows and what it does. Genetic engineers work with DNA to alter the characteristics of plants and animals. For example, they might replace a gene in one species of plant with a gene from another species to make the first plant grow faster or become more resistant to disease. Any new species made like this is known as genetically modified (GM).

◀ The plant below has been altered to make it resistant to the disease that has damaged the plant above.

▲ These pet fish have been genetically altered to make them glow.

WHAT YOU DO

As a genetic engineer you would spend most of your time in a biotechnology laboratory. You would use very specialised equipment and chemicals to analyse samples of DNA, to copy pieces of DNA, to chop up DNA, and to replace genes in cells with genes from other cells. You would also be looking after plants and animals in the lab. Outside the lab, you would keep up-to-date with latest developments in genetic engineering techniques, and even publish you own scientific papers.

THE ROUTE

SCHOOL: Science and maths.

TO GENETIC

SENIOR SCHOOL: Biology, chemistry and maths.

ENGINEERING

UNIVERSITY: A degree in biotechnology, biochemistry or genetics.

WHERE YOU WORK

You have a choice of working for research organisations, universities or biotechnology companies. There are an increasing number of opportunities as the science of genetic engineering becomes more widely used.

▶ This scientist is checking how well a crop of modified corn is growing at a research station.

BRINGING THE PAST TO LIFE

THE STUDY OF EXTINCT SPECIES CAN REVEAL WHAT LIFE WAS LIKE MILLIONS OF YEARS AGO.

Dinosaurology is the study of dinosaurs. It involves unearthing fossil remains and studying them in close detail. It is a brilliant job, but don't get it confused with being a fossil hunter. You might have seen fossil hunters unearthing fabulous dinosaur bones from the desert in TV documentaries, and even in the movies, but dinosaurologists do much more! Dinosaurologists and palaeontologists are experts in the anatomy of plants and animals, and also geology.

A NEW SPECIES OF DINOSAUR IS REVEALED ON AVERAGE EVERY TWO WEEKS, EITHER STRAIGHT OUT OF THE GROUND, OR HIDDEN IN AN OLD COLLECTION.

◄ A scientist prepares a fossil for study.

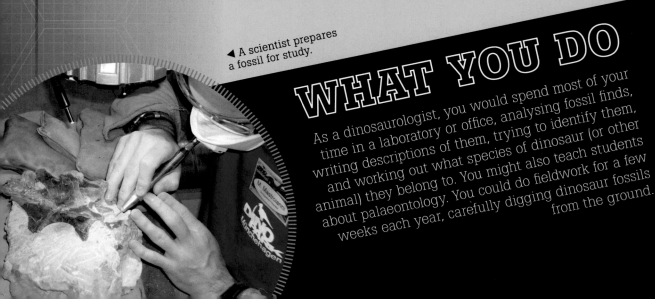

WHAT YOU DO

As a dinosaurologist, you would spend most of your time in a laboratory or office, analysing fossil finds, writing descriptions of them, trying to identify them, and working out what species of dinosaur (or other animal) they belong to. You might also teach students about palaeontology. You could do fieldwork for a few weeks each year, carefully digging dinosaur fossils from the ground.

THE ROUTE TO DINOSAUROLOGY

SCHOOL: Science and an interest in animals.

SENIOR SCHOOL: More science, especially biology, and geography.

UNIVERSITY: A degree in geology, anatomy or earth sciences, along with experience of fieldwork, followed by a doctorate.

WHERE YOU WORK

There are no commercial organisations that employ dinosaurologists, so you would be working for research organisations or universities, helping with research into newly discovered species of dinosaurs.

▲ By studying fossils, scientists can piece together entire skeletons and work out how dinosaurs lived.

DENDROPALAEONTOLOGISTS STUDY THE FOSSILS OF ANCIENT PLANTS. THESE REMAINS TELL US WHAT PLANTS LIVED ON THE EARTH IN THE PAST, AND GIVE US AN IDEA OF HOW THE EARTH MIGHT HAVE LOOKED.

RUN FASTER!

THIS JOB HELPS ATHLETES TO RUN FASTER, JUMP HIGHER AND PERFORM AT THEIR VERY BEST.

A biomechanist can make a difference to the performance of athletes. Even small changes in technique can be the difference between winning and losing. Biomechanists understand not only mechanics, but also bones, joints and muscles, and how they work together. They apply this specialist knowledge to help athletes move more efficiently, so they can run and swim faster, throw further and jump higher. They also work out how athletes get injured, and help athletes to avoid getting injured in the first place.

◀ Improving her technique means that this athlete can jump even further.

◀ Analysing an athlete's gait, or stride, can improve a runner's speed and efficiency.

WHAT YOU DO

As a biomechanist you would spend some of your day in a lab, studying athletes with specialist equipment, such as high-speed cameras to study how a person moves and measuring tools to gauge the strength and performance of different muscles. You would analyse results and advise athletes on how to improve their techniques.

▲ A special underwater camera used to record the motion and technique of swimmers.

▲ Motion tracking highlights how different parts of this swimmer move with each stroke.

THE ROUTE TO BIOMECHANICS

SCHOOL: Science, maths and an interest in sports

SENIOR SCHOOL: More science and maths

UNIVERSITY: A degree in biomechanics, followed by a masters or doctorate to get top jobs

WHERE YOU WORK

There are opportunities for biomechanists to work for individual athletes and sports teams. These might even be elite athletes and professional teams. You would normally work hand-in-hand with other specialists, including nutritionists, sports psychologists and physiotherapists. Sports equipment companies also use biomechanists to help design exercise equipment.

◀ This equipment, known as an ergospirometry laboratory, can check how efficiently an athlete's body operates, by monitoring the lung capacity and heart rate.

ATOM SMASHER

▼ When particles smash into each other, they break up into tiny particles that can be detected by the sensors.

BY SMASHING THINGS APART, THIS JOB COULD HELP YOU UNCOVER THE SECRETS OF THE UNIVERSE.

Particle physicists smash atoms apart in an attempt to discover what exactly stuff is made from. There are two types of particle physicist: theoretical particle physicists and experimental particle physicists. The theoretical ones come up with theories about what particles they think exist, and the experimental ones develop experiments to test the theories!

▼ Physicists at the Large Hadron Collider study data after a collision.

WHAT YOU DO

As a theoretical particle physicist, you would spend your time in an office at a university, using computer models, pen and paper, to work on theories. You might also lecture, passing on your expertise to students. As an experimental particle physicist, you would spend some days operating experiments. Other days will be spent analysing results and writing reports, or developing and building new experimental machines.

WHERE YOU WORK

All particle physicists work for universities or research organisations. You might work as part of a team that is researching a particular problem, and the work could take many years. As an experimental physicist, you would work at an experimental facility, such as the Large Hadron Collider (LHC) in Switzerland and France.

UNIVERSITY: A degree in physics or astrophysics, followed by research and a master's degree or doctorate in particle physics

THE CIRCULAR TUNNEL AT THE LARGE HADRON COLLIDER HAS A CIRCUMFERENCE OF 27 KM.

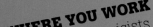

SENIOR SCHOOL: Science, especially physics and chemistry, and further maths

THE ROUTE TO PARTICLE PHYSICS

SCHOOL: Science and maths

◄ Tiny atoms are sent along the tunnels at close to the speed of light.

◄ The large tunnel of the LHC runs underground on the border between France and Switzerland.

GLOSSARY

ANTHROPOLOGIST
A person who studies human culture, including our origins, religious beliefs and how we relate socially with each other.

ATOMS
A tiny particle that is usually made up of a nucleus containing protons and neutrons, with one or more electrons whizzing around these.

BIOMECHANICS
The study of how living things move about, including how people walk, run and jump.

BIOTECHNOLOGY
Using tiny organisms, such as bacteria, to carry out chemical changes, such as producing medicines or food.

COSMONAUT
The Russian name given to a person who travels into space.

DNA
Short for deoxyribonucleic acid, this strand-like chemical is found inside cells and contains the code which tells the cell how to grow and behave.

DOCTORATE
One of the highest qualifications you can receive.

DORMANT VOLCANO
A volcano that hasn't erupted for a period of time, but that might erupt at some point in the future.

EXOPLANET
A planet that orbits a star other than our Sun.

EXPERT WITNESS
A person who is specialised in a particular subject and gives his or her expert opinion in a court.

FIELDWORK
The collection of data outside of a classroom, laboratory or office.

GAIT
How a person walks or runs.

GENES
Made out of DNA, a gene dictates a specific characteristic, such as how a person behaves or looks.

GENETICALLY MODIFIED
When the genes of an organism have been altered to change one of its characteristics.

GPS
Short for Global Positioning System, this is a network of satellites in orbit around Earth, which a person can use, along with a receiver, to locate their position.

HURRICANES
Huge tropical storms.

MAGMA
Liquid rock that swirls beneath Earth's surface in a layer called the mantle.

MASTER'S DEGREE
A university degree that is a higher level than a first, or bachelor's, degree.

METEOROLOGIST
A person who studies the weather and how it is created by events in Earth's atmosphere.

MOTION TRACKING
Following and recording the movement of an object or parts of a person's body to see how they behave.

NERVOUS SYSTEM
The system of nerve cells that carry small electrical signals around an organism. It also includes the spinal cord and brain.

NEUROSURGEON
A person who performs surgery on a patient's nervous system.

NUTRITIONAL INFORMATION
The data, usually found on packaging, which tells you what nutrients are found inside food.

PALAEONTOLOGIST
A scientist who studies the fossil remains of long-dead plants and animals to find out how they lived and what conditions were like when they were alive.

PROSECUTED
When someone has been charged with a criminal act and taken to court

RADAR
A system to locate objects, such as planes and boats, which uses a beam of radio signals and detects the echoes of this beam to calculate the location.

SEISMOMETER
Also called a seismograph, this is a device which records earthquakes, measuring their magnitude.

SPACE AGENCY
An organisation that sends robot or crewed missions into space.

TORNADOES
Powerful storms that form funnel-shaped clouds as they spin around violently.

TRANSPLANT
In surgery, this is the removal of one body part that is sick or has stopped working, and replacing it with a new part that has usually been taken from a person who has died recently.

UNDERGRADUATE
A person who is studying at a university for their first degree.

VOLCANOLOGIST
A scientist who studies volcanoes and their eruptions.

INDEX

Published in paperback in Great Britain
in 2019 by Wayland
Copyright © Hodder and Stoughton, 2016
All rights reserved

Editor: Victoria Brooker
Produced by Tall Tree Ltd
Editor: Jon Richards
Designer: Darren Jordan

ISBN: 978 0 7502 9995 4
10 9 8 7 6 5 4 3 2 1

Wayland
An imprint of Hachette
Children's Group
Part of Hodder and Stoughton
Carmelite House
50 Victoria Embankment
London EC4Y 0DZ

An Hachette UK Company
www.hachette.co.uk
www.hachettechildrens.co.uk

Printed and bound in China

The website addresses (URLs) included in this
book were valid at the time of going to press.
However, it is possible that contents or addresses
may have changed since the publication of this
book. No responsibility for any such changes can
be accepted by either the author or the Publisher.

MIX
Paper from
responsible sources
FSC
www.fsc.org
FSC® C104740